Rainbow FRIENDS

A Tale of Friendship and Understanding

Cari Rawling

Write and Release
PUBLISHING

www.writeandreleasepublishing.com

For Mark, Gage, Jayden, and Sam—your love and encouragement guide me every day. And to all the children I've been blessed to know, thank you for the joy and inspiration.

In a preschool just like ours, a vibrant group of friends exists, each as unique as the colours of the rainbow.

There is Emma,
an artist at heart,
who loves to paint
with all the colours
of the world.

Liam finds joy in building tall towers out of colourful blocks, and Maya loves to dance to the rhythm of the music.

In this preschool, there is also a friend named Alex. Alex has a very good memory and loves following routines. Alex knows a lot about Dinosaurs and enjoys talking about them with everyone.

Alex sees the world in a way that is different from the other children. Sometimes, loud noises make Alex cover his ears, bright lights make him squint and busy rooms overwhelm him.

On a bright and sunny day, the friends were out on the playground. Emma brought a splash of colours to life, painting a vibrant rainbow on a large canvas.

Nearby, Liam constructed towering structures with colourful blocks, while Maya twirled and danced beautifully. Meanwhile, Alex carefully built a cozy home for his dinosaurs.

However, when the playful shouts and fast-paced running of his friends filled the air, Alex began to feel a bit overwhelmed. Maya noticed that Alex seemed anxious and asked, "Are you okay, Alex?" Alex shook his head and said, "Loud noises make me feel a bit scared."

The friends quickly understood and decided to play quietly. They gathered together, taking turns sharing their favourite activities. Emma painted, Liam built with blocks, Maya danced gracefully, and Alex enthusiastically shared fascinating facts about Dinosaurs.

As they shared and listened to one another, they discovered each other's uniqueness. They celebrated their differences, recognizing how extraordinary each one was, just like the colours of a rainbow.

From that day on, the friends embraced the importance of thinking about everyone's needs. They adapted their activities, sometimes engaging in busy loud play, while other times exploring art, constructing towers, learning about dinosaurs, and dancing in perfect harmony.

Whenever they played lively games, Alex, mindful of his sensitivity, used headphones to make the sounds quieter, ensuring everyone could play together.

And so, in this preschool, they all became rainbow friends, all learning that being different is what makes them special. They treasure each other's unique qualities and celebrate the beauty of their diversity, just like the many colours of a rainbow.

With hearts full of understanding and kindness, they continue their colourful journey of friendship, creating a world where every day is filled with laughter, play and the warmth of acceptance.